Alfred's Top 50 SONGS
FROM THE WARNER BROS. FILM COLLECTION

Warner Bros. continues to entertain the world with films passionately produced, selectively acquired, carefully preserved and impeccably curated for both the casual and ultimate movie lover to enjoy forever. As a result of all the films the studio has produced, co-produced (with numerous partners), acquired and distributed, Warner Bros. now boasts the largest film library in the world—6,800 feature films. Warner Bros. Entertainment is also home to a massive catalogue of music copyrights from the films in this library. Alfred Music presents the sheet music to several of those wonderful titles in this collection.

Produced by
Alfred Music
P.O. Box 10003
Van Nuys, CA 91410-0003
alfred.com

Printed in USA.

ISBN-10: 1-4706-2058-8
ISBN-13: 978-1-4706-2058-5

MOVIE INDEX

CONTENTS BY TITLE

ADELIELAND

(from *Happy Feet*)

Composed by
JOHN POWELL

Moderately bright latin ♩ = 132

Adelieland - 3 - 1

6

ALL IS LOVE
(from *Where the Wild Things Are*)

Words and Music by
KAREN O and NICK ZINNER

AMERICA'S AVIATION HERO
(from *The Aviator*)

Composed by
HOWARD SHORE

Moderately (♩ = 88)

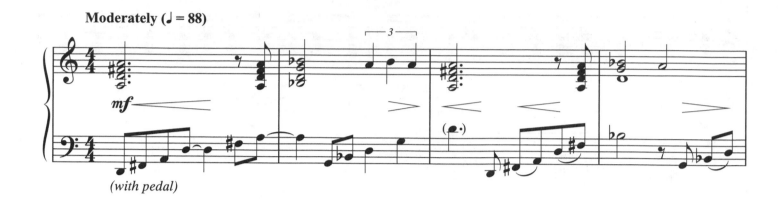

(with pedal)

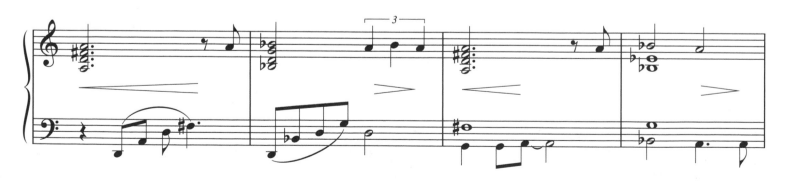

America's Aviation Hero - 2 - 1

ARTHUR'S THEME
(BEST THAT YOU CAN DO)

(from *Arthur*)

Words and Music by
BURT BACHARACH, CAROLE BAYER SAGER,
CHRISTOPHER CROSS and PETER ALLEN

Arthur's Theme (Best That You Can Do) - 4 - 1

16

Arthur's Theme (Best That You Can Do) - 4 - 3

AUGUST RUSH (PIANO SUITE)

(from *August Rush*)

Composed by
MARK MANCINA
Arranged by DAVE METZGER

Gently (♩. = 54)
"Main Theme"

August Rush (Piano Suite) - 5 - 1

Delicately (♩ = 80) "August's Theme"

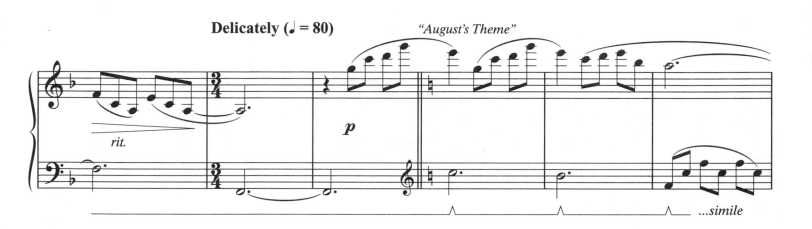

rit.   p   ...simile

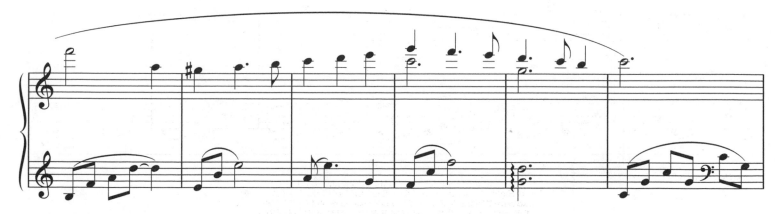

(a bit more deliberately)

"Parents Theme"

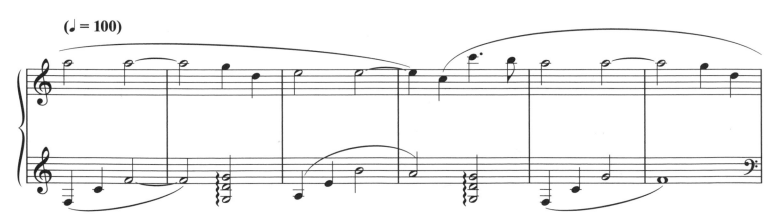

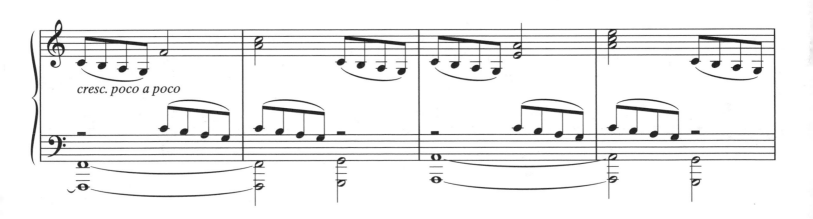

"August's Rhapsody"

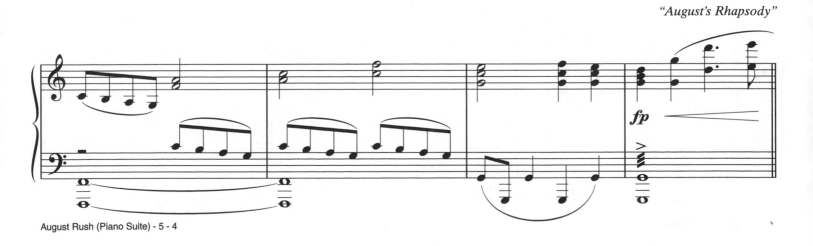

August Rush (Piano Suite) - 5 - 4

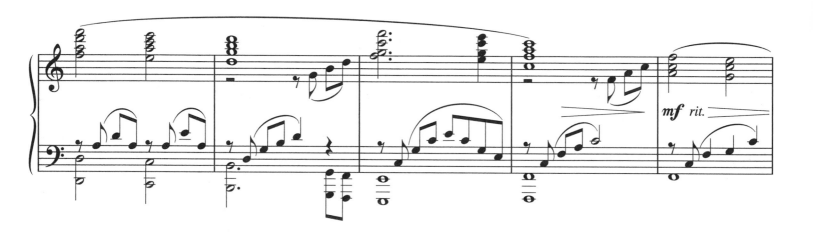

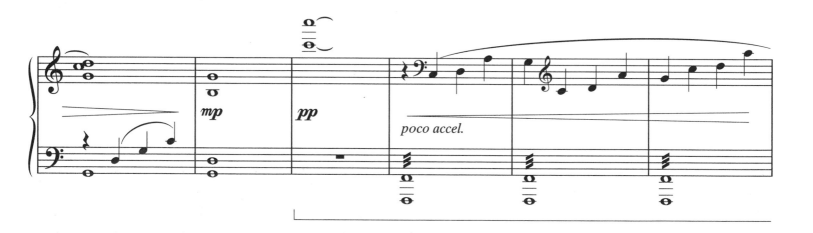

BILLY'S THEME

(from *The Departed*)

Composed by
HOWARD SHORE

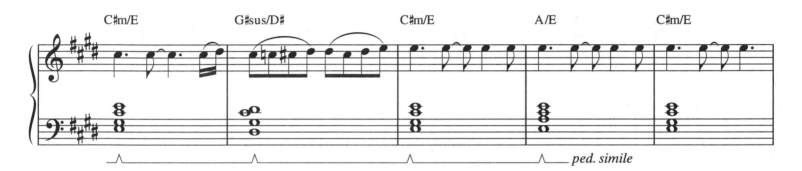

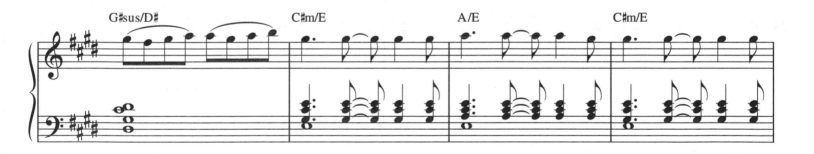

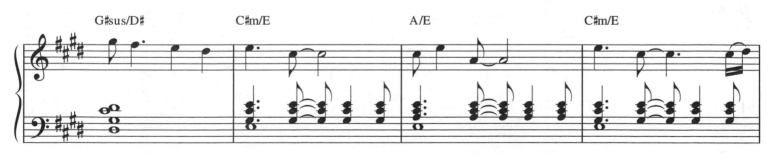

Billy's Theme - 7 - 1

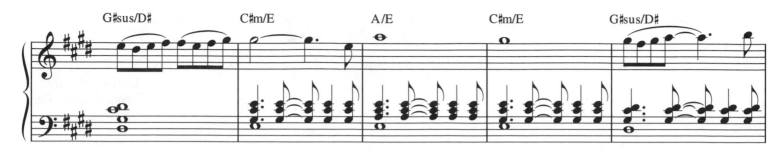

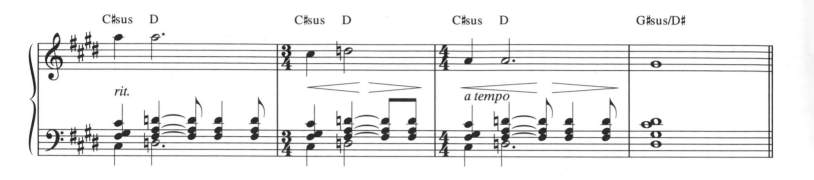

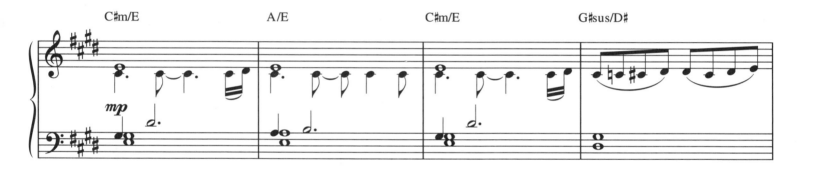

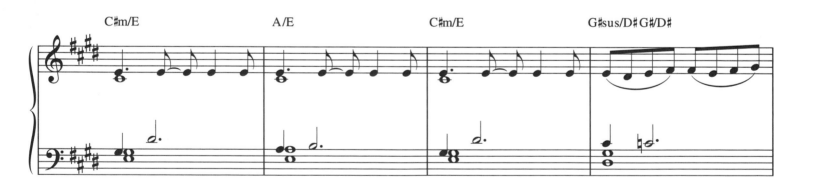

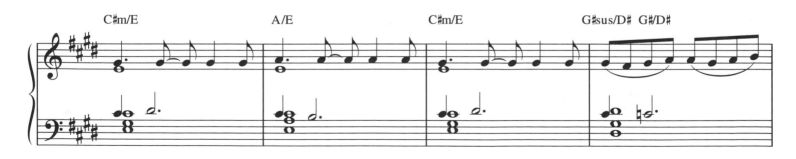

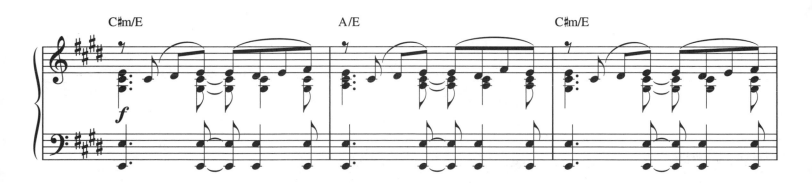

Billy's Theme - 7 - 3

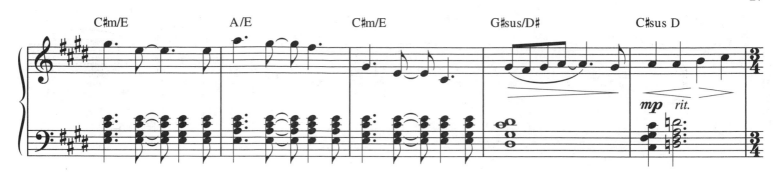

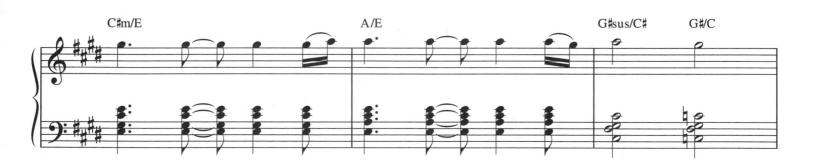

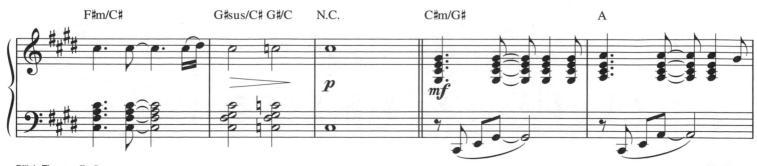

Billy's Theme - 7 - 5

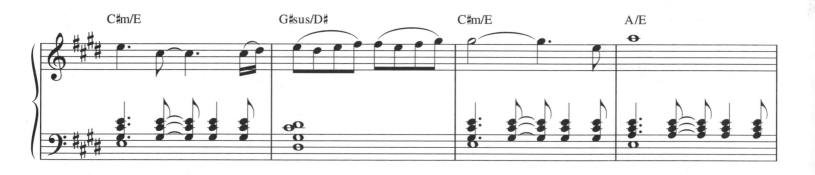

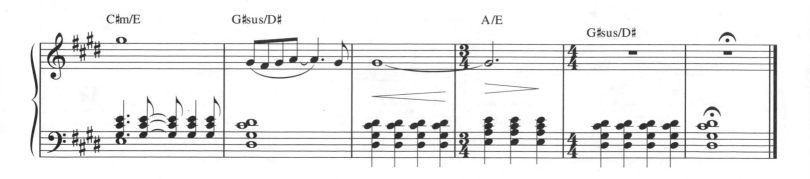

Billy's Theme - 7 - 7

BATMAN FOREVER

(from *Batman Forever*)

Words and Music by
ELLIOT GOLDENTHAL

Main Title
Rubato ♩ = 66

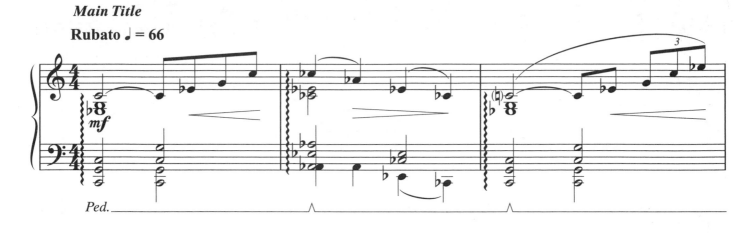

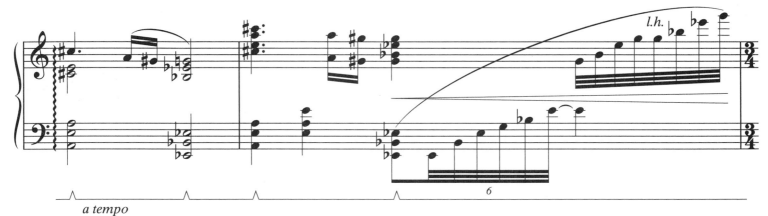

Batman Forever - 4 - 1

Più mosso ♩ = 80

rit.

Fast ♩ = 144

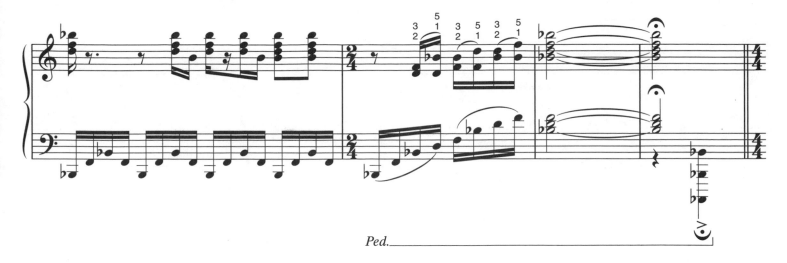

Rooftop Seduction Theme

Sultry and sensuous ♩ = 78

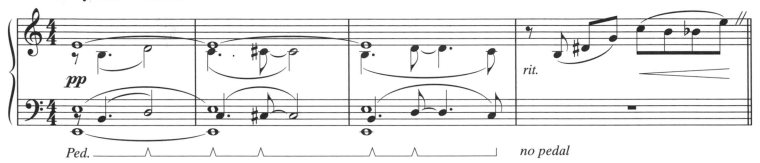

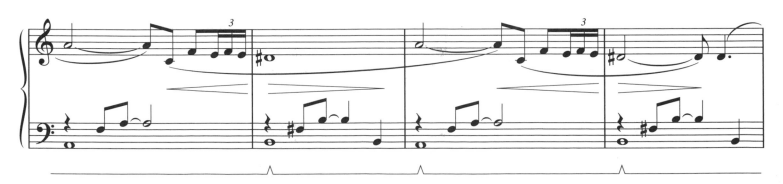

BELIEVE
(from *The Polar Express*)

Words and Music by
ALAN SILVESTRI and GLEN BALLARD

Moderately slow ♩ = 80

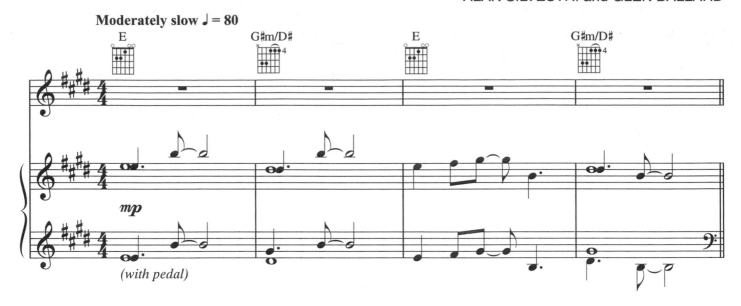

(with pedal)

Verse:

1. Chil - dren___ sleep - ing,___ snow is soft - ly fall - ing.___
2. Trains move___ quick - ly___ to their jour - ney's end.

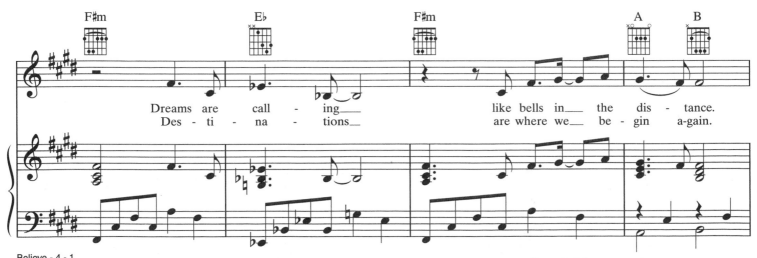

Dreams are call - ing___ like bells in___ the dis - tance.
Des - ti - na - tions___ are where we___ be - gin a - gain.

Believe - 4 - 1

Repeat ad lib. and fade

CAN YOU READ MY MIND?

(from *Superman*)

Words by
LESLIE BRICUSSE

Music by
JOHN WILLIAMS

COME SO FAR (GOT SO FAR TO GO)

(from *Hairspray*)

Lyrics by
SCOTT WITTMAN and
MARC SHAIMAN

Music by
MARC SHAIMAN

Come So Far (Got So Far to Go) - 9 - 1

46

Come So Far (Got So Far to Go) - 9 - 6

CONCERNING HOBBITS

(from *The Lord of the Rings: The Fellowship of the Ring*)

By
HOWARD SHORE

Moderately (♩ = 104)

Warmly (legato)

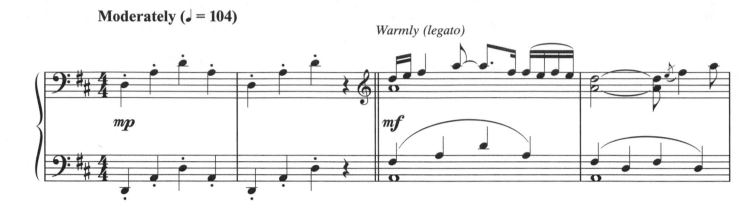

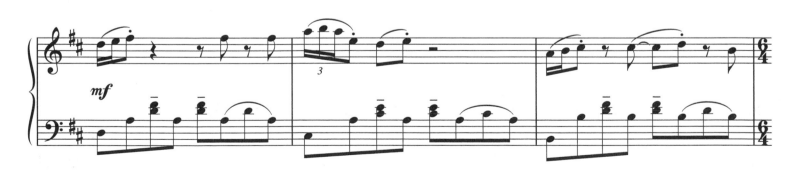

52

Warmly (legato)

CORYNORHINUS
(from *Batman Begins*)

Composed by
**HANS ZIMMER, JAMES NEWTON HOWARD,
MELVYN WESSON, RAMIN DJAWADI
and LORNE BALFE**

Moderately slow, rubato (♩ = 72)

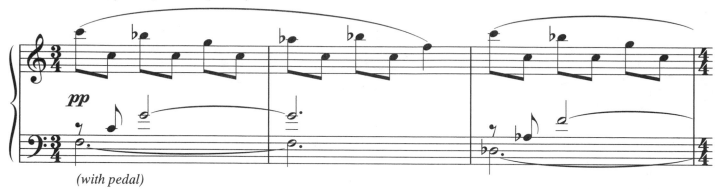

(with pedal)

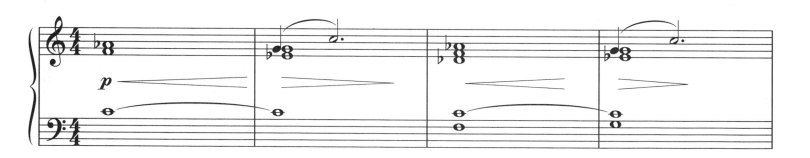

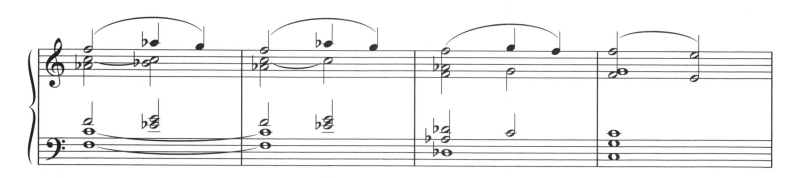

Corynorhinus - 3 - 1

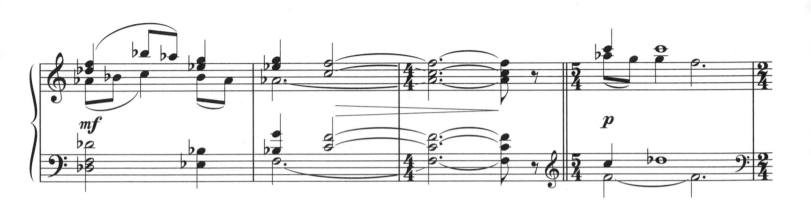

Corynorhinus - 3 - 2

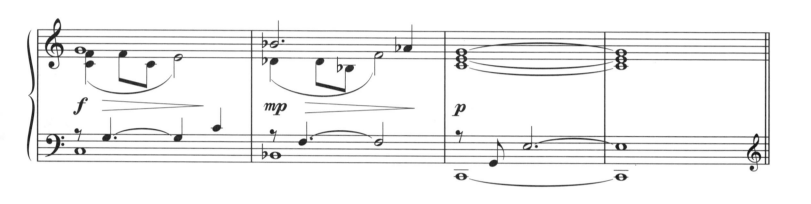

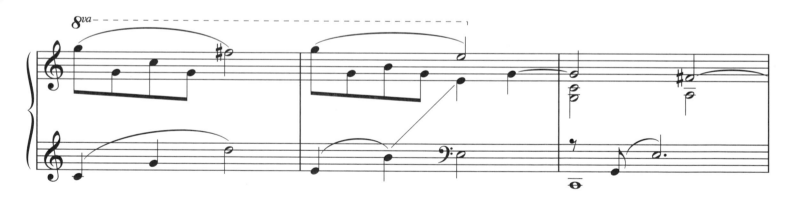

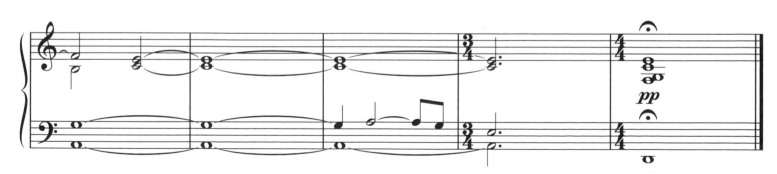

THE DARK KNIGHT OVERTURE

(from *The Dark Knight*)

Composed by
HANS ZIMMER
and JAMES NEWTON HOWARD

Mysteriously (♩ = 96)

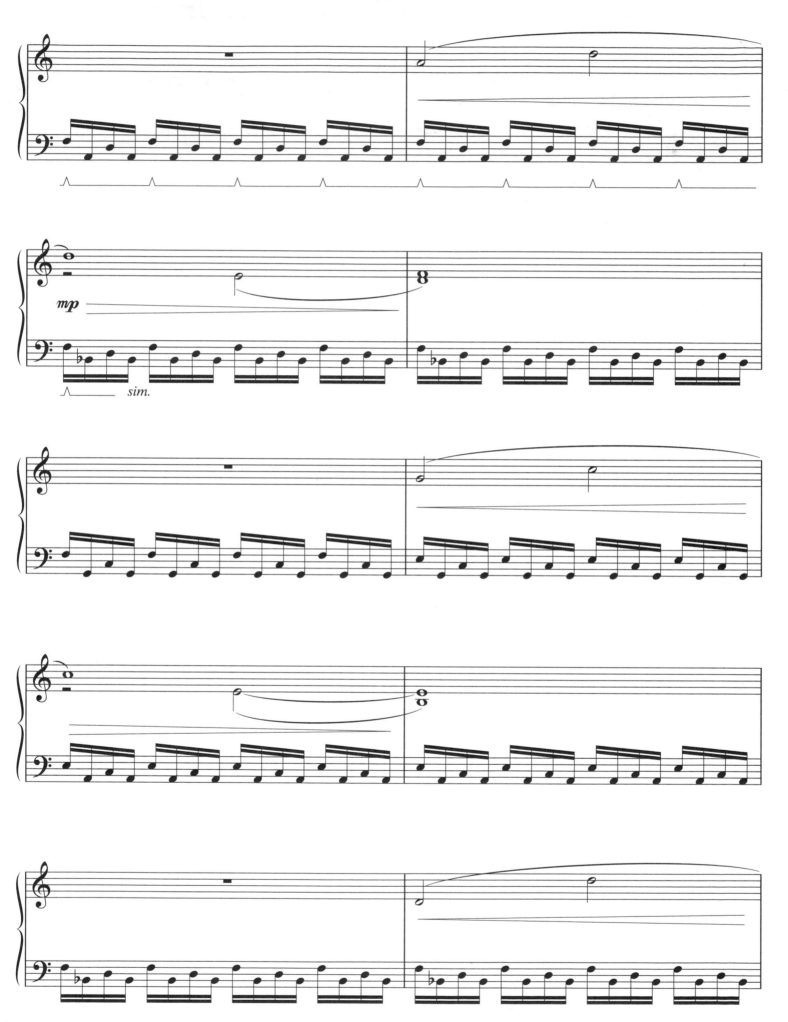

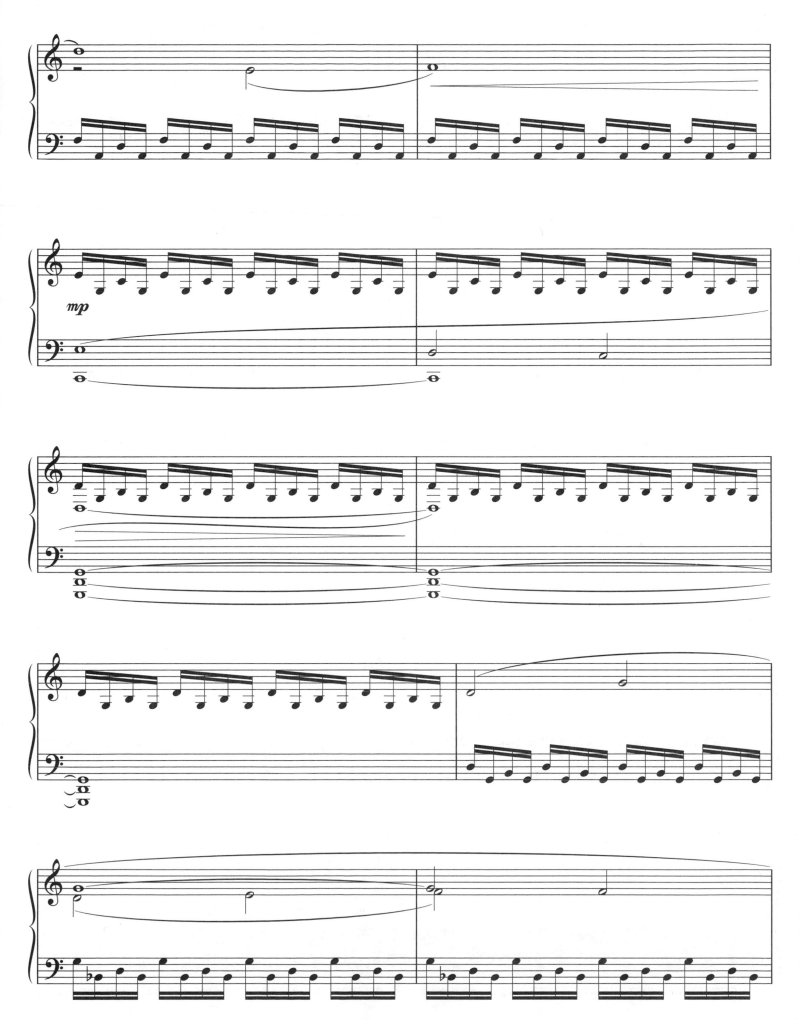

64

68

THE DEPARTED TANGO

(from *The Departed*)

Composed by
HOWARD SHORE

Moderately ♩ = 120

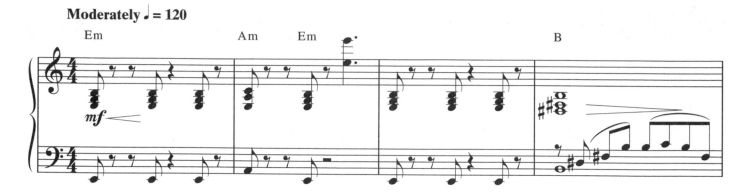

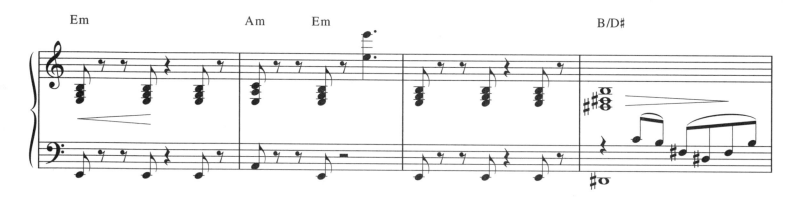

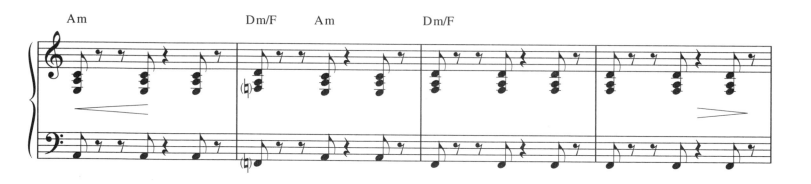

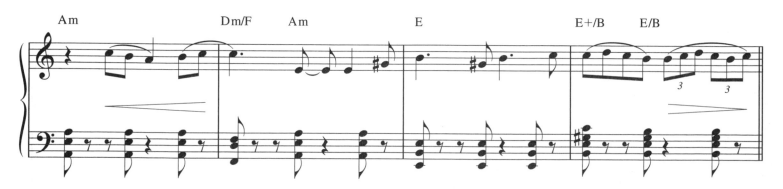

The Departed Tango - 3 - 1

72

DISCOMBOBULATE

(from *Sherlock Holmes*)

Composed by
HANS ZIMMER

Slowly (♩ = 72)

Twice as fast (♩ = 142)

Discombobulate - 5 - 1

DREAM IS COLLAPSING

(from *Inception*)

Composed by
HANS ZIMMER

Mysterious march (♩ = 120)

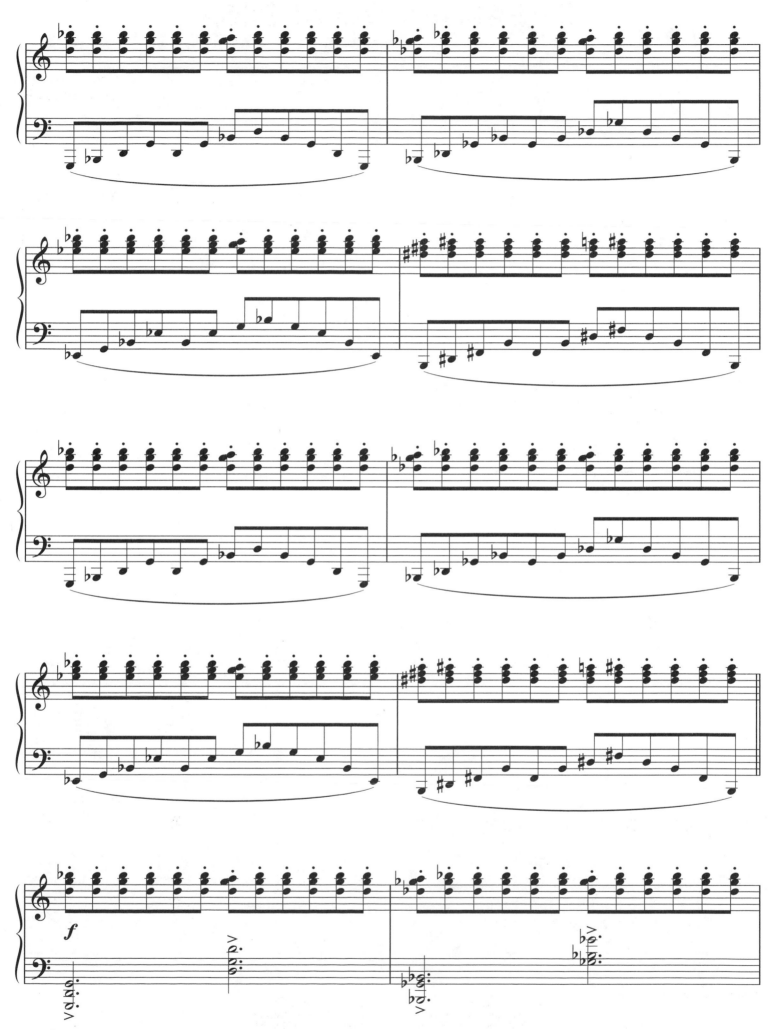

Slower (♩ = 112)

EVERGREEN
(from *A Star Is Born*)

Words by
PAUL WILLIAMS

Music by
BARBRA STREISAND

Moderately, with feeling

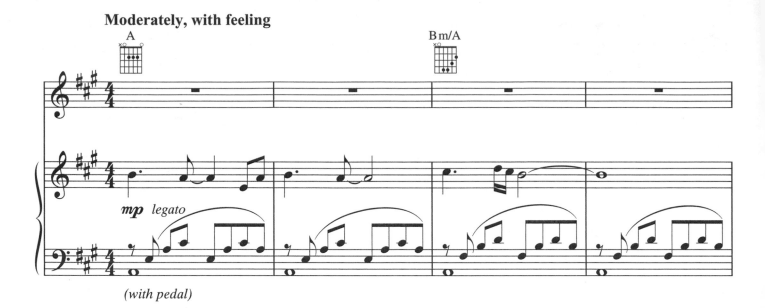

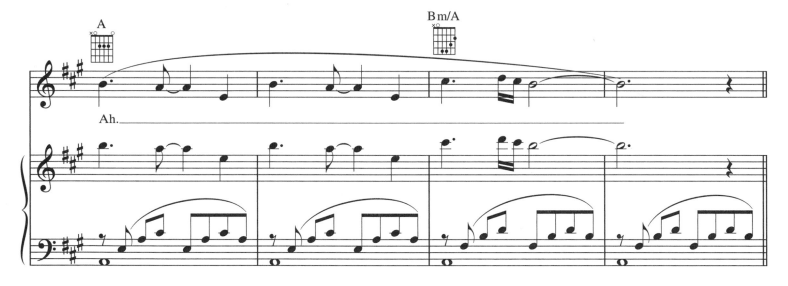

Ah.

Love,_____ soft as an eas - y chair;_____

Evergreen - 6 - 1

88

EXTREMELY LOUD & INCREDIBLY CLOSE
(MAIN THEME)

(from *Extremely Loud & Incredibly Close*)

Composed by
ALEXANDRE DESPLAT

Gently (♩ = 158)

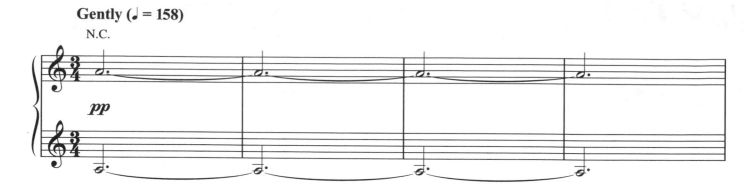

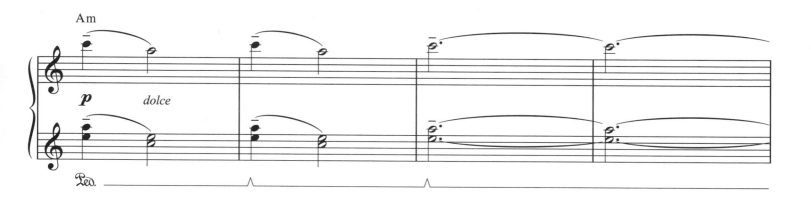

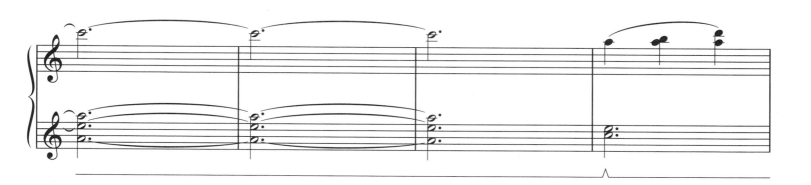

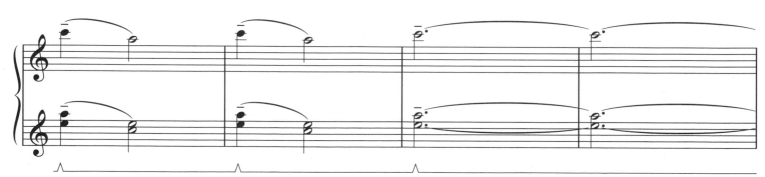

Extremely Loud & Incredibly Close (Main Theme) - 5 - 1

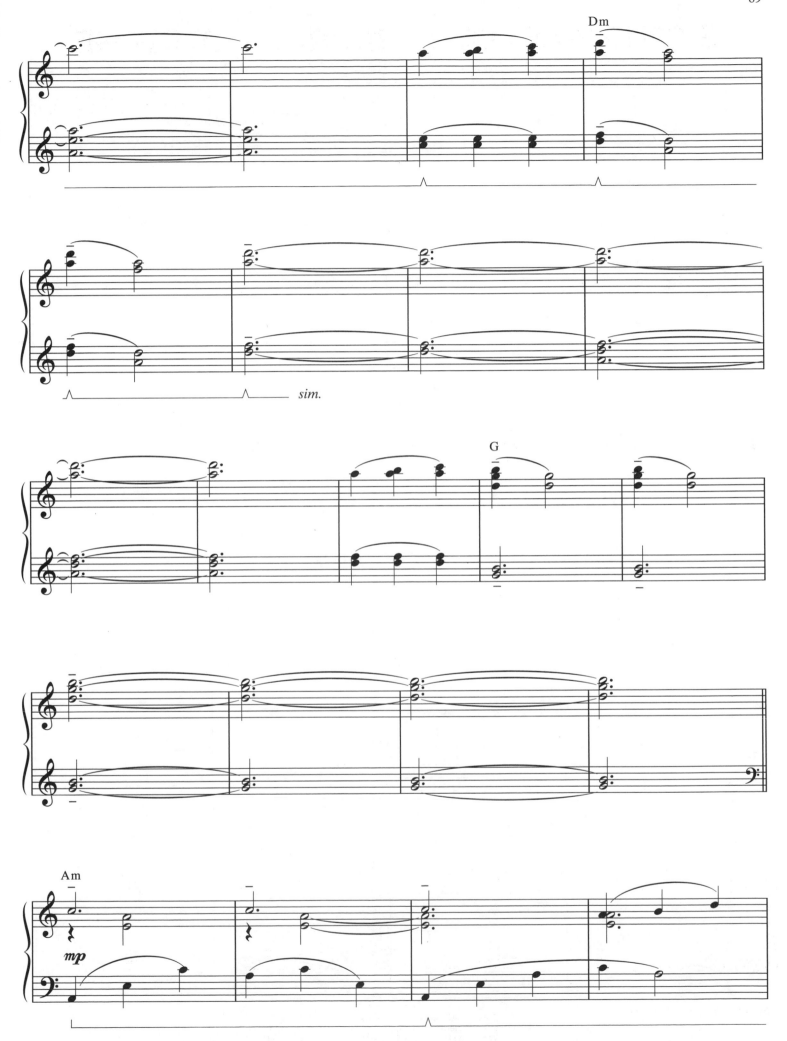

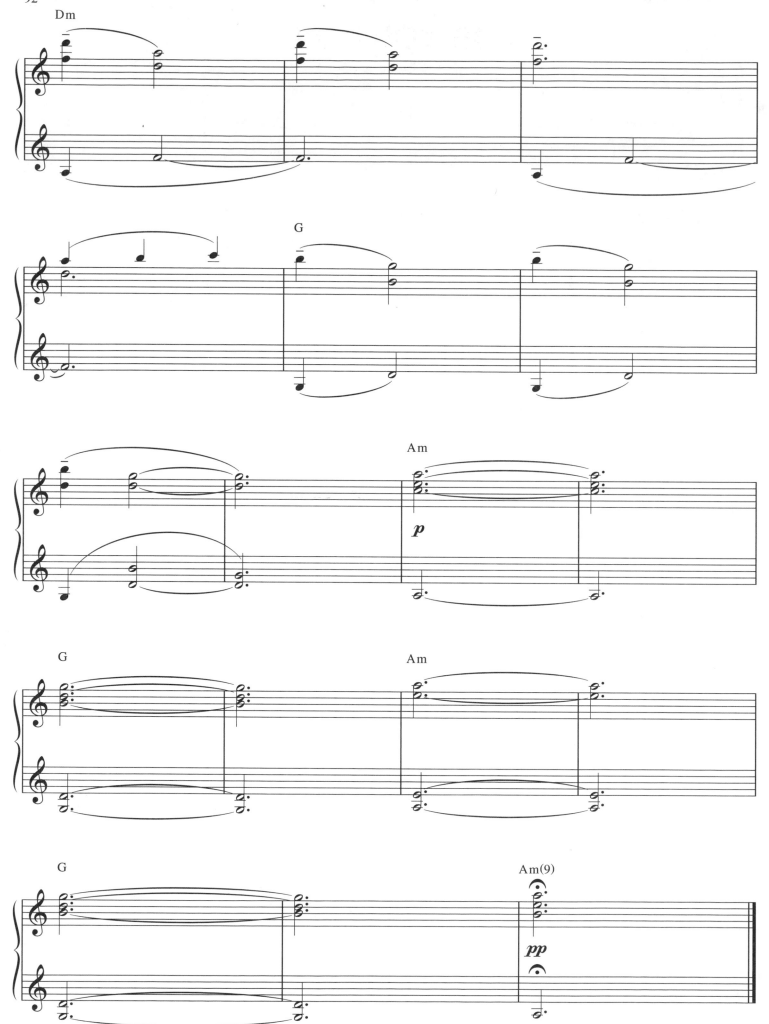

FOR YOU I WILL

(from *Space Jam*)

Words and Music by
DIANE WARREN

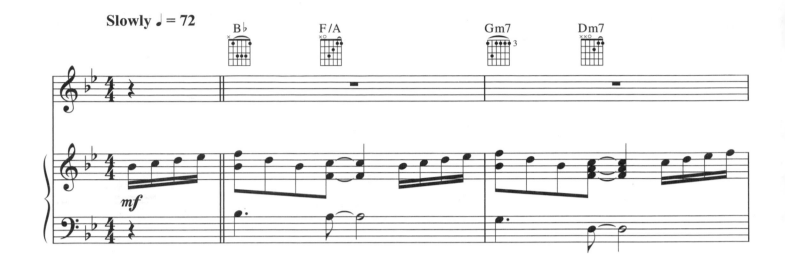

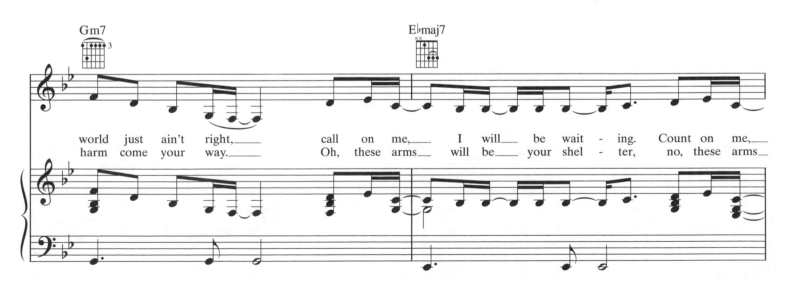

For You I Will - 5 - 1

Chorus:

FLIGHT
(from *Man of Steel*)

Composed by
HANS ZIMMER

Moderately slow (♩ = 80)

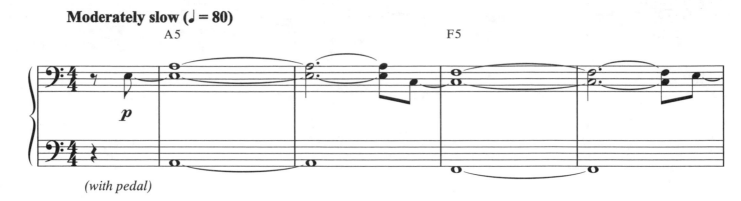

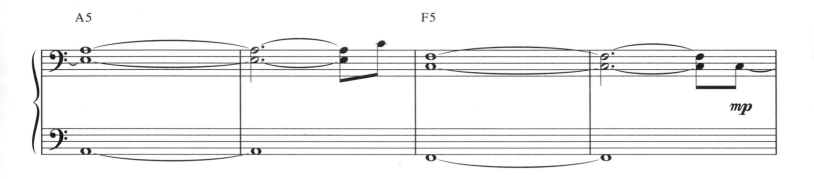

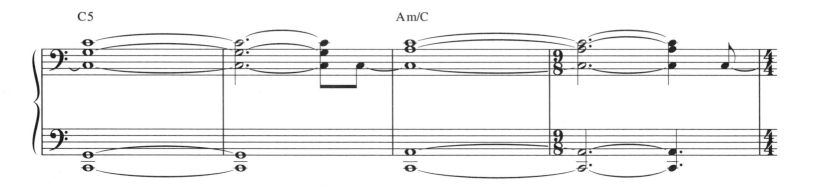

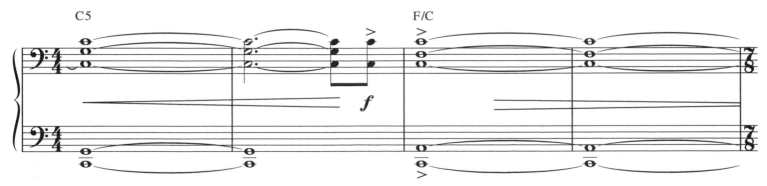

Flight - 4 - 1

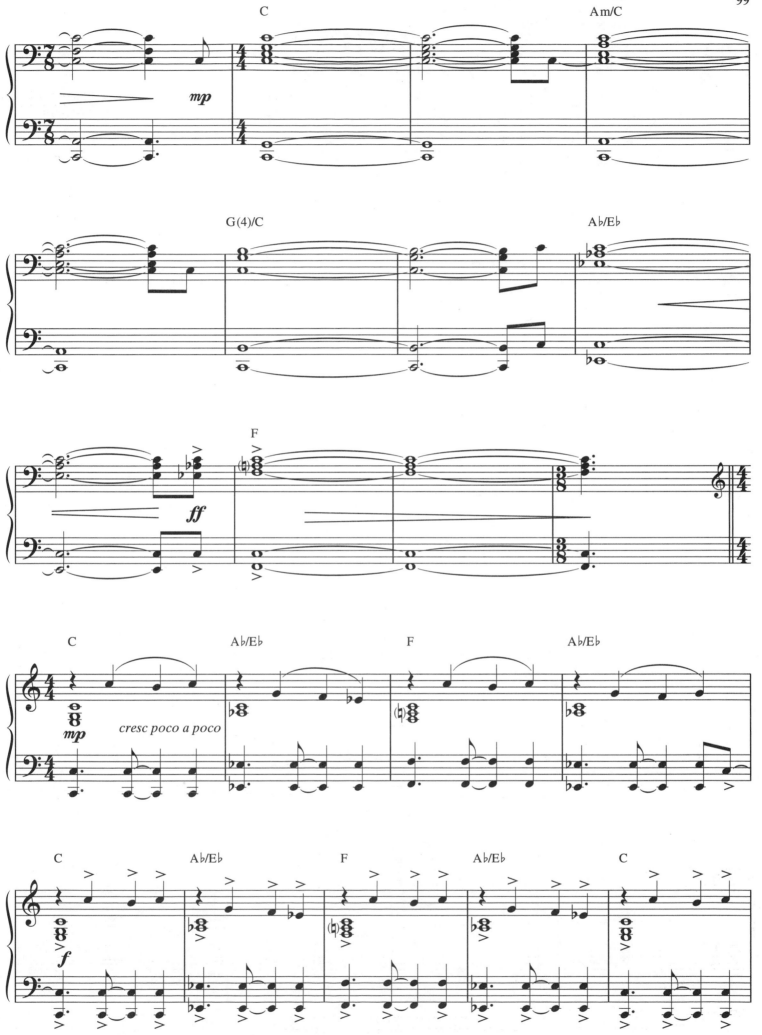

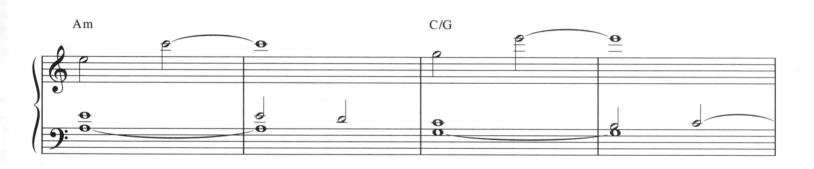

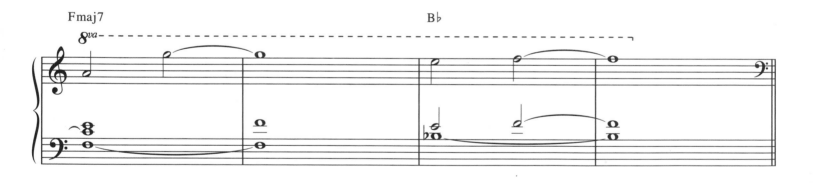

GODZILLA! (MAIN TITLE THEME)
(from *Godzilla*)

Composed by
ALEXANDRE DESPLAT

Moderately ♩ = 100

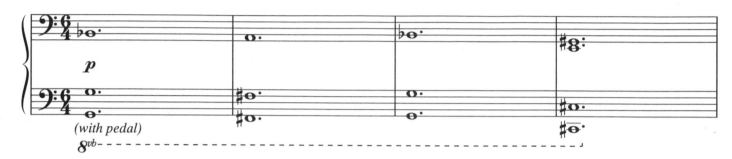

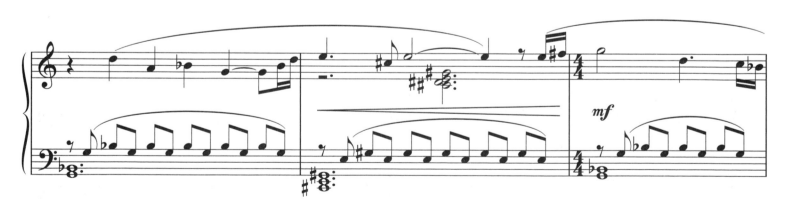

Godzilla! (Main Title Theme) - 4 - 1

104

GOLLUM'S SONG

(from *The Lord of the Rings: The Two Towers*)

Words by FRAN WALSH
Music by HOWARD SHORE

Gollum's Song - 5 - 1

GRAVITY

(from *Gravity*)

Composed by
STEVEN PRICE

Moderately ♩ = 92

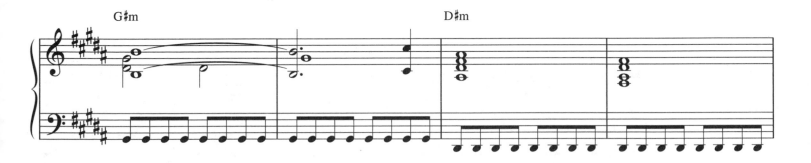

Gravity - 3 - 1

THE HARSHEST PLACE ON EARTH
(OPENING THEME)

(from *March of the Penguins*)

Composed by
ALEX WURMAN

Moderately slow ♩ = 80

The Harshest Place on Earth (Opening Theme) - 3 - 1

The Harshest Place on Earth (Opening Theme) - 3 - 2

116

HEDWIG'S THEME

(from *Harry Potter and the Sorcerer's Stone*)

Composed by
JOHN WILLIAMS

Misterioso ♩. = 58

(with pedal)

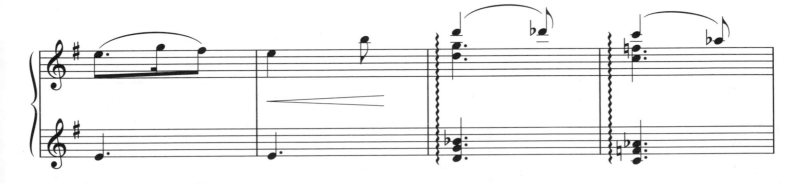

Hedwig's Theme - 5 - 1

Hedwig's Theme - 5 - 3

120

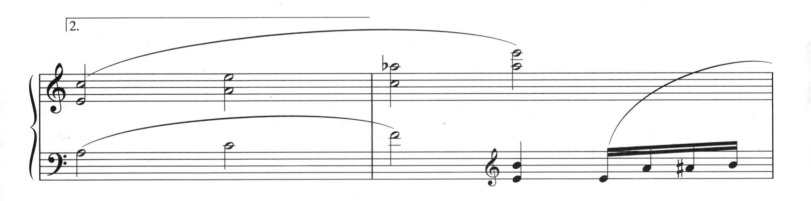

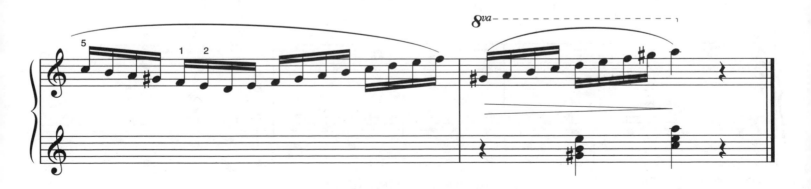

Hedwig's Theme - 5 - 5

HOW DO YOU KEEP THE MUSIC PLAYING?

(from *Best Friends*)

Lyrics by
ALAN and MARILYN BERGMAN

Music by
MICHEL LEGRAND

Moderate ballad

How do you keep the mu-sic play-ing?

How do you make it last? How do you keep the song from fad-ing too fast?

How Do You Keep the Music Playing? - 5 - 1

126

IN DREAMS

(from *The Lord of the Rings: The Fellowship of the Ring*)

Words and Music by
FRAN WALSH and
HOWARD SHORE

In Dreams - 3 - 1

INTO THE WEST

(from *The Lord of the Rings: The Return of the King*)

Words and Music by
HOWARD SHORE, FRAN WALSH, ANNIE LENNOX

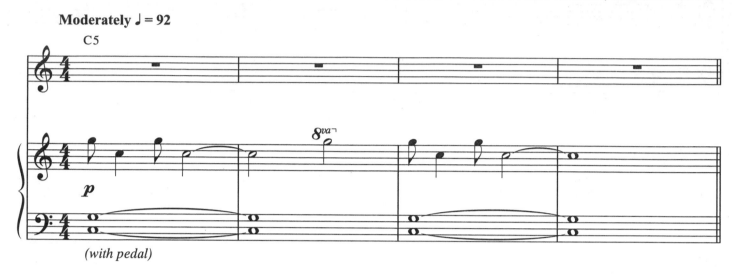

Into the West - 7 - 1

Why do the white gulls call?_____

A - cross the sea,

a pale moon ris - es. The ships have

come to car - ry you home._____

134

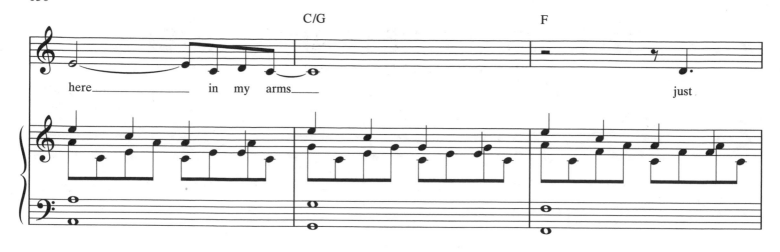

here_____ in my arms_____ just

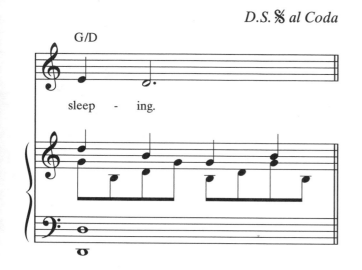

D.S. 𝄋 *al Coda*

sleep - ing.

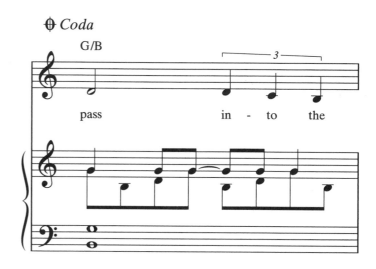

𝄌 *Coda*

pass in - to the

West._____

rit. e dim.

THE LUCKY ONE (MAIN THEME)

(from *The Lucky One*)

Composed by
MARK ISHAM

Gently, in 2 ♩ = 150 (♩. = 50)

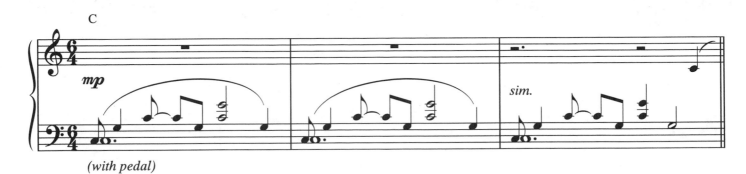

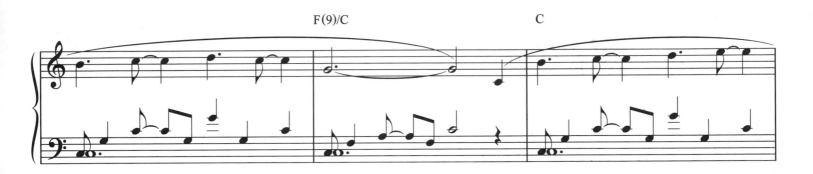

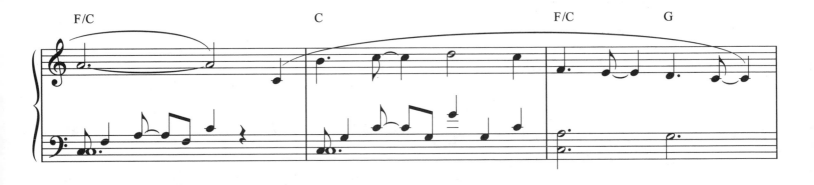

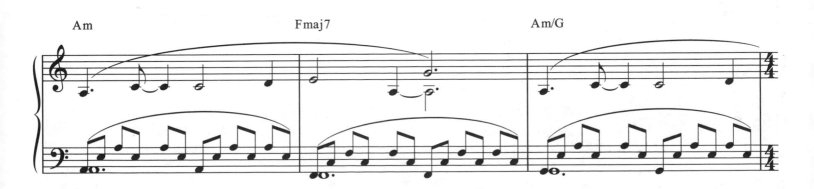

The Lucky One (Main Theme) - 3 - 1

138

The Lucky One (Main Theme) - 3 - 3

LYRA

(from *The Golden Compass*)

Words and Music by
KATE BUSH

Where are our lives_____ if there is no dream? Where is our

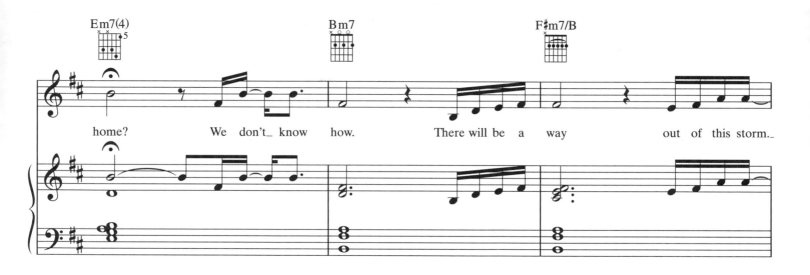

home? We don't_ know how. There will be a way out of this storm._

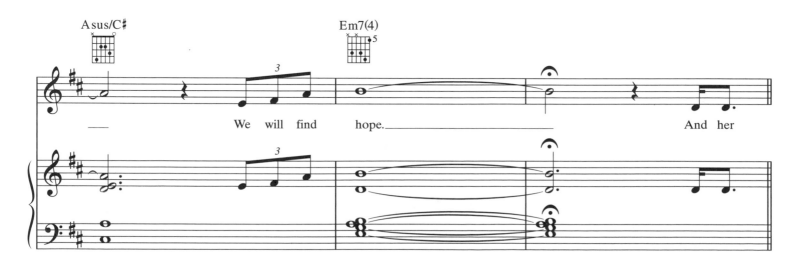

We will find hope._____ And her

THE MISSION

(from *Argo*)

Composed by
ALEXANDRE DESPLAT

Maestoso (♩ = 76)

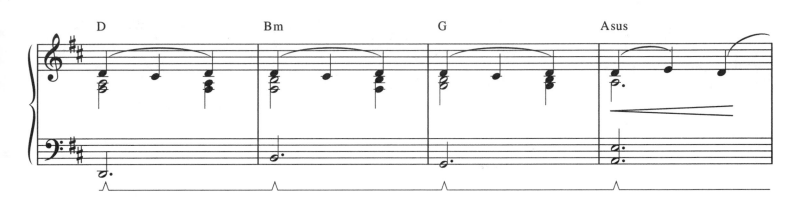

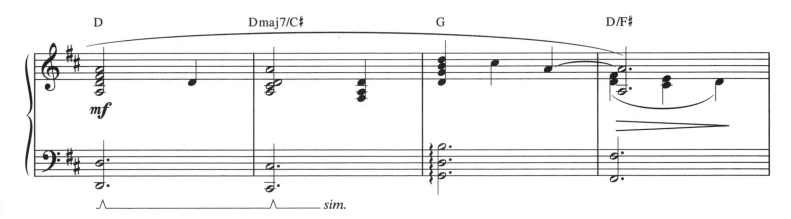

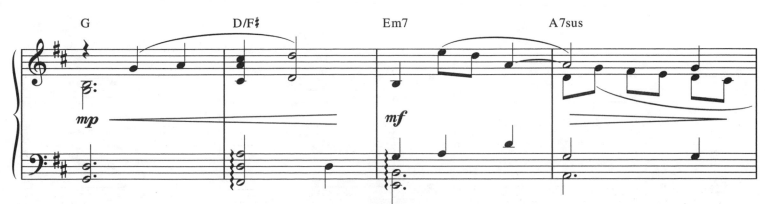

The Mission - 3 - 1

144

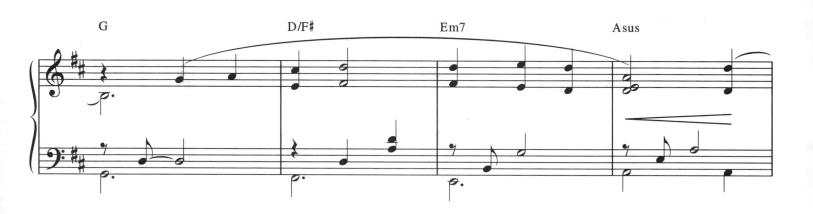

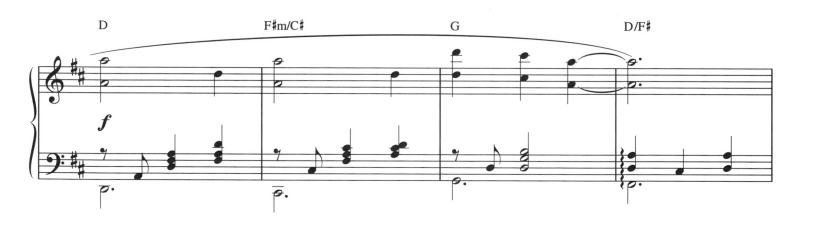

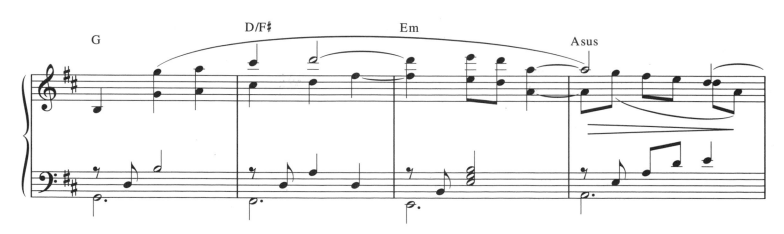

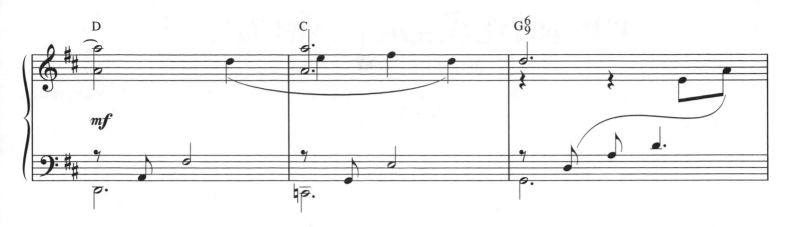

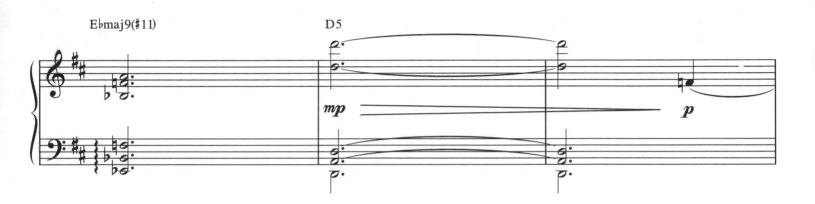

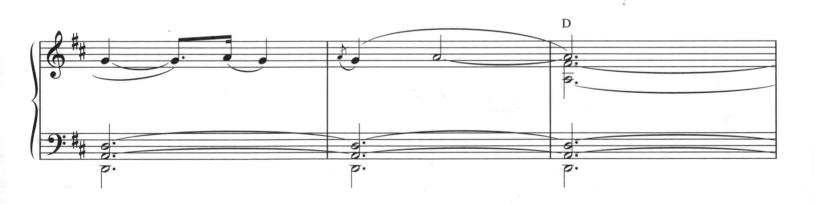

The Mission - 3 - 3

THE NOTEBOOK (MAIN TITLE)
(from *The Notebook*)

Written by
AARON ZIGMAN

Slowly, with expression ♩ = 58

Più mosso

A little faster ♩ = 69

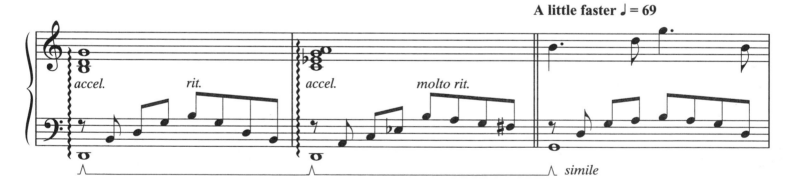

The Notebook (Main Title) - 3 - 1

148

The Notebook (Main Title) - 3 - 3

OVER THE RAINBOW

(from *The Wizard of Oz*)

Lyrics by
E.Y. HARBURG

Music by
HAROLD ARLEN

THE POSEIDON (MAIN TITLE)

(from *Poseidon*)

Composed by
KLAUS BADELT

The Poseidon (Main Title) - 3 - 1

SOME FUN NOW

(from *Little Shop of Horrors*)

Words by
HOWARD ASHMAN

Music by
ALAN MENKEN

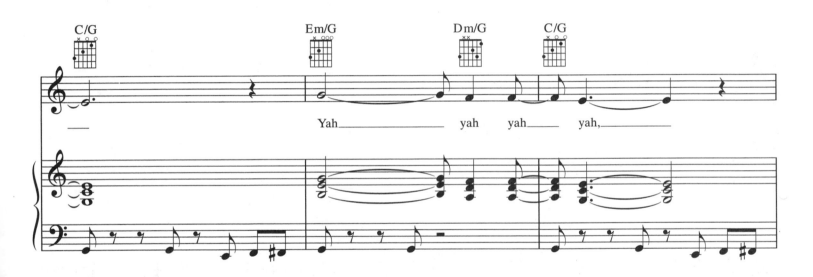

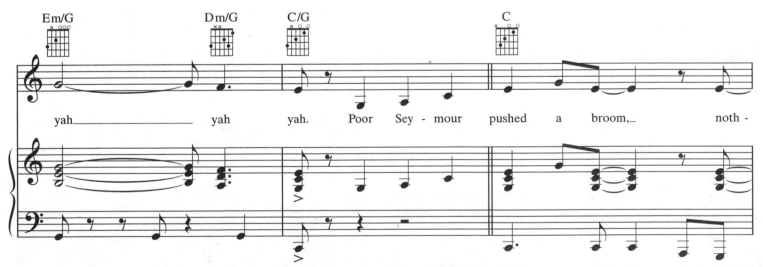

Some Fun Now - 5 - 1

156

Some Fun Now - 5 - 3

158

THE PRAYER

(from *Quest for Camelot*)

Italian Lyric by
ALBERTO TESTA and TONY RENIS

Words and Music by
CAROLE BAYER SAGER and DAVID FOSTER

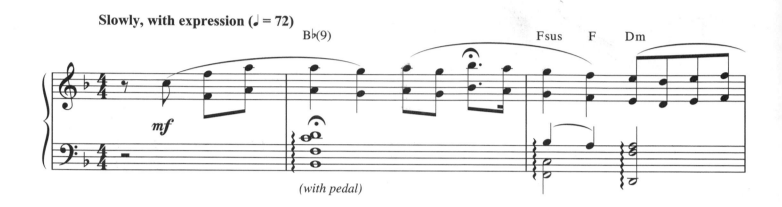

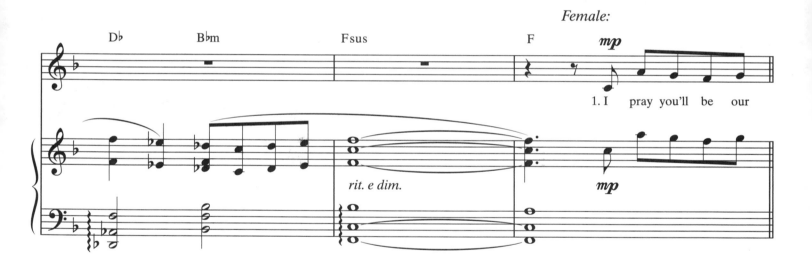

PURE IMAGINATION

(from *Willy Wonka & the Chocolate Factory*)

Words and Music by
LESLIE BRICUSSE and
ANTHONY NEWLEY

Moderately, with expression (♩ = 120)

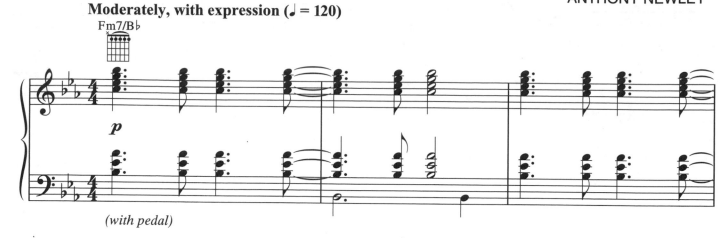

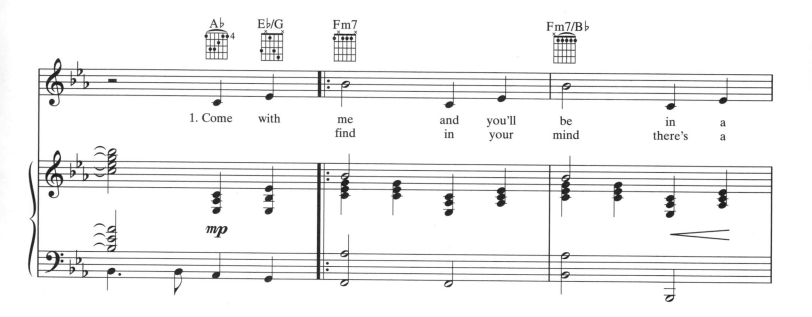

1. Come with me and you'll be in a
find in your mind there's a

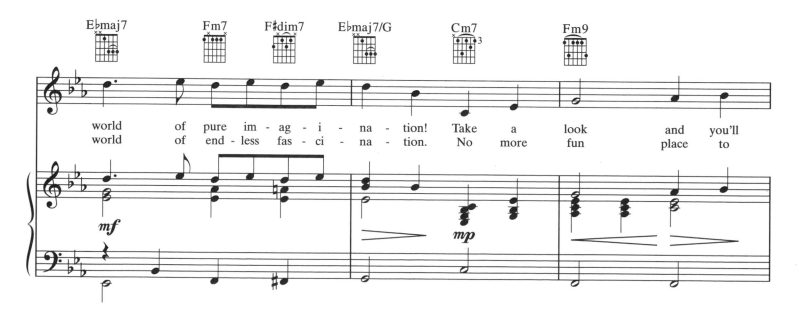

world of pure im-ag-i- na- tion! Take a look and you'll
world of end-less fas-ci- na- tion. No more fun place to

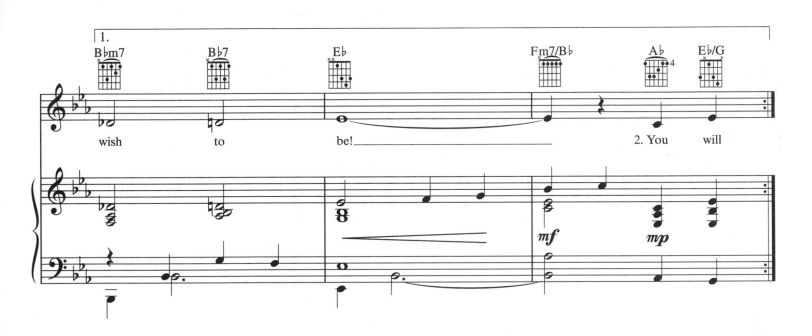

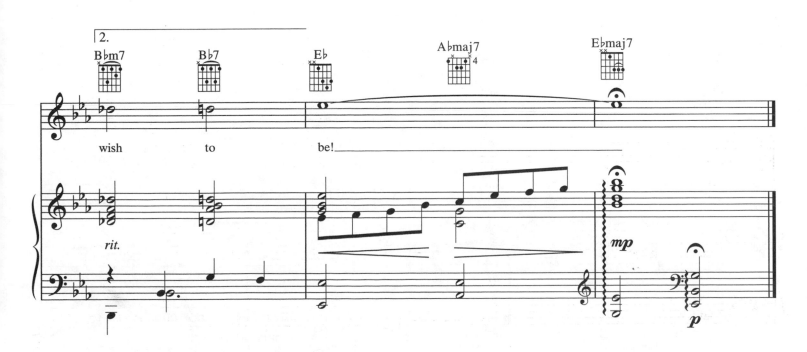

REMEMBER ME

(from *Troy*)

Lyrics by
CYNTHIA WEIL

Music by
JAMES HORNER

Remember Me - 6 - 1

Verse:

1. I _____ am the one star _____ that keeps burn - ing _____ so bright - ly, _____ it is the
2. I _____ am that warm voice _____ in the cold wind _____ that whis - pers, _____ and if you

(2nd time:) Ah, _____

THE RETURN OF THE KING

(from *The Lord of the Rings: The Return of the King*)

Music by HOWARD SHORE
Contains the Composition *Aragorn's Coronation*
Melody by VIGGO MORTENSEN
Lyrics by J.R.R. TOLKIEN

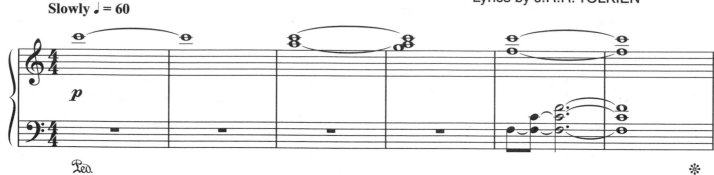

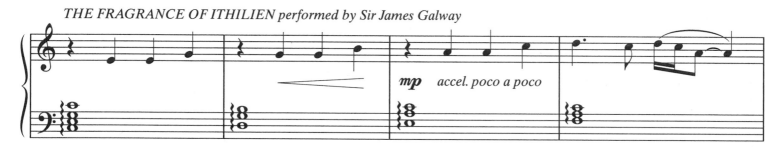

ARAGORN'S CORONATION *performed by Viggo Mortensen*

Solo: Et Eär-el-lo En-do-ren-na u-tú-li-en

Si - no - me ma-ru-van ar Hil di

Choir: En Si

nyar   tenn´   Am - bar - me_____ ta._____

ny_____   Am_____ ta.____   Hmm.

QUEEN ARWEN SONG performed by Renée Fleming

Slightly faster ♩ = 72

Solo: Ti_____   nú_____   vi_____   el____

182

Choir: Hmm

Hmm

A TOAST IN THE SHIRE
performed by Dermot Crehan

Faster ♩ = 112

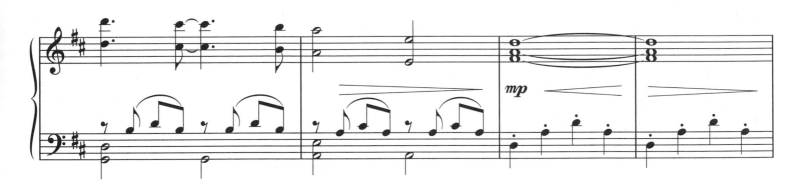

ARAGORN'S CORONATION
Out of the Great Sea to Middle-Earth I am come.
In this place will I abide, and my heirs, unto the ending of the world.

ARWEN - (first appearance)
Tinuviel the elven fair
Immortal maiden elven wise
About him cast her shadowy hair
And arms like silver glimmering

ROHAN

(from *The Lord of the Rings: The Two Towers*)

Composed by
HOWARD SHORE

Rohan - 2 - 1

Slower ♩ = 63
THE KING OF THE GOLDEN HALL

SECONDHAND LIONS (MAIN THEME)

(from *Secondhand Lions*)

By
PATRICK DOYLE

March ♩ = 120

Smoothly

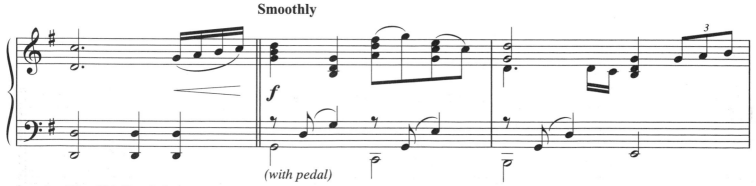

(with pedal)

Secondhand Lions (Main Theme) - 2 - 1

a little slower

SINGIN' IN THE RAIN

(from *Singin' in the Rain*)

Lyric by
ARTHUR FREED

Music by
NACIO HERB BROWN

To Coda ⊕

lane with a hap - py re - frain, and sing - in',___ just sing - in' in___ the

rain._____

Why   am   I   smil - in',   and
Why   do   they   call   me   and   the

why   do   I   sing?___   Why   does   De - cem - ber   seem
boy   with   the   smile?___   When   did   I   find   out   that

sun - ny   as   spring?___   Why   do   I   get   up   each
life   is   worth - while?___   Why   do   I   treat   all   my

SOMEWHERE MY LOVE
(LARA'S THEME)

(from *Doctor Zhivago*)

Lyric by
PAUL FRANCIS WEBSTER

Music by
MAURICE JARRE

Lyrics:
Some - where, my love, there will be songs to sing, al - though the snow cov - ers the hope of spring. Some - where a hill

Somewhere My Love (Lara's Theme) - 3 - 2

198

THE SUMMER KNOWS

(from *The Summer of '42*)

Lyrics by
ALAN and MARILYN BERGMAN

Music by
MICHEL LEGRAND

The Summer Knows - 3 - 1

THEME FROM SUPERMAN

(from *Superman*)

Composed by
JOHN WILLIAMS

Theme from Superman - 4 - 1

(♩. = ♩)

mp

4/4

4/4

Theme from Superman - 4 - 2

Theme from Superman - 4 - 4

THE SWEETHEART TREE

(from *The Great Race*)

Words by
JOHNNY MERCER

Music by
HENRY MANCINI

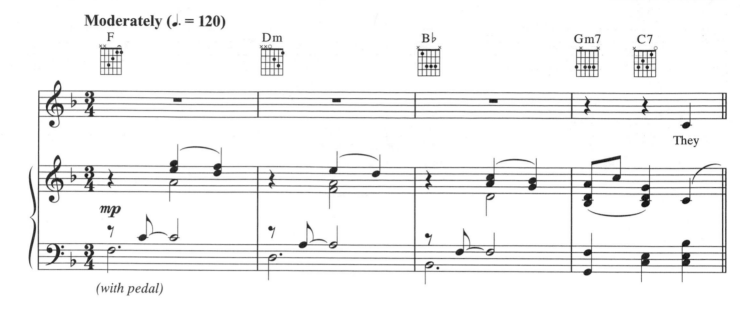

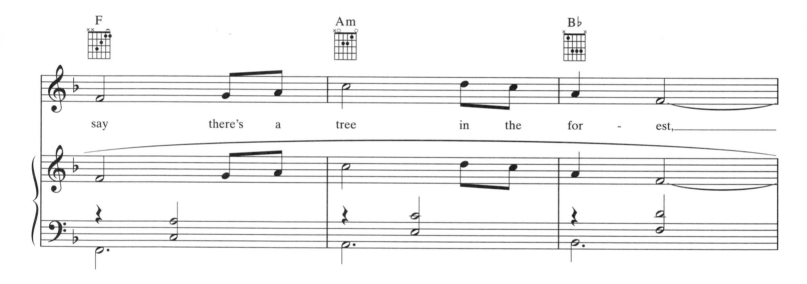

The Sweetheart Tree - 3 - 1

SYRIANA THEME

(from *Syriana*)

Composed by
ALEXANDRE DESPLAT

Syriana Theme - 3 - 1

TIME

(from *Inception*)

Composed by
HANS ZIMMER

Slowly (♩ = 60)

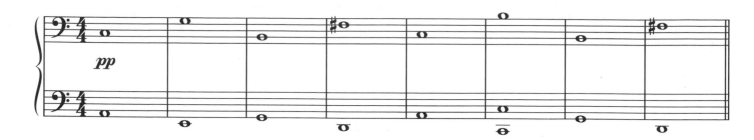

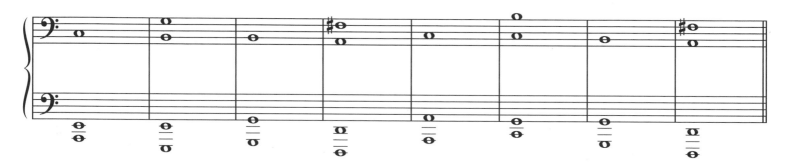

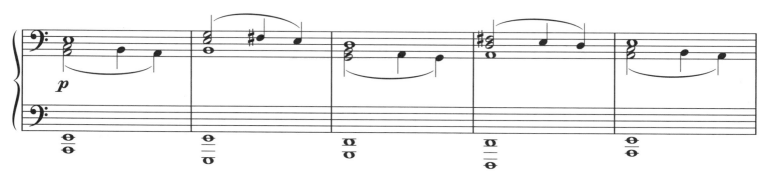

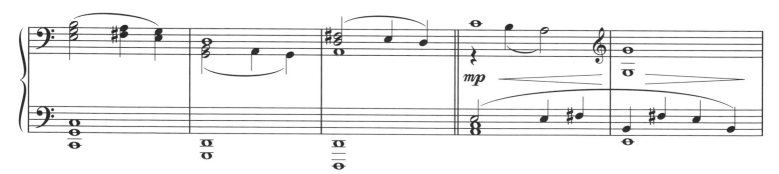

Time - 3 - 1

WONKA'S WELCOME SONG

(from *Charlie and the Chocolate Factory*)

Lyrics by
JOHN AUGUST and DANNY ELFMAN

Music by
DANNY ELFMAN

WAY BACK INTO LOVE

(from *Music and Lyrics*)

Words and Music by
ADAM SCHLESINGER

Way Back Into Love - 7 - 1

F: Oh._____

M: Whoa._____

F: Oh,___ oh.___

M: Oh,___ oh.___

M: Oh, oh._

F: Oh._____